To Mom, Dad, and Ronald — for making Orange County the place I call "home."

To Buddy, my long-time teddy bear — for listening to my screams of angst.

Prologue: O Come, All Ye Basics

Orange County is a great place to grow up and a great place to die.

It's an ideal location to both participate in youth soccer and to while away the end of your days protesting high-density housing.

Welcome, with all the glazed-over warmth that a Southern Californian can muster, to my comprehensive consideration of "What is the OC?" No, not the show. That was so 2004. What? No, not that show either. All housewives are real! I think.

If you're holding this book in your hands, you likely fall into one of four categories:

1. **An Orange County native who got the hell out.** You simultaneously have sweet memories of those wide, paved lanes while having PTSD about the constant remodeling.

    Q: "Mom, why are we retiling the floor *again*?!"
    A: "Because we can."

If you fall into this first category, good for you for breaking out of the Orange Curtain! Especially if you are someone in the age range of 18-70. Come back when you are ready to die.

2. **A proud Orange County native. Born and raised, baby.**

If you fall into this second category, I understand. Orange County excels in many things, including our beaches and our racism. However, be warned. This book takes a very honest look at the 714/949. If you can't handle the snark, I suggest returning to your prescription medication.

3. **A tourist wishing to learn more about Orange County** before traveling here for Disneyland and/or the sex trafficking rings.

If you are of the third category, then I am sorry you paid money to read this. Please enjoy anyway. Also note, dear tourist: Los Angeles (an hour north of the OC) and Orange County are two entirely separate entities. LA is like the kid in high school who left home to pursue a rap career, only to end up in vegan catering. Orange County is the kid who never left home, only to end up in family real estate.

4. **Someone who has purchased or been gifted this book so you may truly understand what it means to be from the OC.**

If you are of this last category, you will benefit the most. Within these pages is an unapologetic examination of a peculiar suburban microcosm of the United States. Of course, the tale that lies within is particular to one humble Millennial. One humble, self-involved Millennial who anticipates offending a lot of people with her opinions on her hometown.

This book is structured with anecdotes, pictures of OC folk doing OC things, and quotes lifted from real conversations. An OC Native's Guide to politics, Disneyland, and raising your child are peppered throughout. If you skipped this prologue and are just now coming back with some confusion as to "is this real life?", the answer is yes — this is satire.

Technically, this is a parody of Brandon Stanton's "Humans of New York." But let's be real. Orange County is a parody of Orange County.

Welcome to suburbia. Welcome to the lives of scores of white people, many Asian people, tons of Hispanic people, and six black people.

Welcome to Orange County, CA.

A convo with an OC real estate agent:
"$1 million is not going to do a lot for you. Unless you want to end up in the ghetto."

OC Native's Guide to Orange County Cities

Anaheim: Home to Disneyland and Disney's version of municipal governance. Anaheim is oodles of fun, if your wallet can handle it.

Costa Mesa: Home to South Coast Plaza, Orange County's OG shopping destination.[1] SCP is the West Coast's largest shopping center, a billion-dollar retail machine, and one of the many monstrosities people in the 1800s imagined in dystopian futures.

You know how people travel to see Rome's Colosseum or Greece's Acropolis? Three hundred years from now, when Orange County has fallen into dissolution, tourists will flock to visit the "Ruins of Orange County": our freeway system and SCP.

"Centuries ago, people came here to purchase ironic D.A.R.E. t-shirts for $19.99 from a store called Forever 21! Isn't it quaint how they thought their love for Jesus would sustain them for eternity?"

Garden Grove/Westminster: Home to the second largest Vietnamese population in the United States, Garden Grove and Westminster are an endless series of strip malls, each guaranteed to contain a pho restaurant and a doctor's office. Twenty-four–hour pho is a thing here, and it is the greatest gift GG/W has given humanity.[2]

Huntington Beach: Home to the International Surf Competition and white people. Lots of white people.

Irvine: A city swaddled in upper middle class wealth and suburban psychosis.

Someone once told me Irvine was the most planned city in America. Every tree, lane, and road has been calculated to maximize suburban bliss. If you drive from one end of Irvine to the other, it all looks the same. It's Stepford made real, but with a lot more Asian immigrants.

Irvine is the kind of place where a parent would demand a school ban on watermelons because her child is allergic to them. The administration would reply, "Ma'am, there are no school activities in Southern California requiring watermelon consumption."

---

[1] OG may stand for Original Gangsta, Olive Garden, or Obama's Gonads. OG is used in reference to mean "the original," although I wish we would discuss the state of Barack's gametes more often.
[2] Pho is pronounced "fuh," making for delightful restaurant names such as "Pho King" and "Pho Me."

"What is wrong with you people?" she'd yell. "You are psychologically traumatizing my child! I'll be seeing you in court."

"Wait, this isn't rational," the flustered administrator would say. That is where the administrator is mistaken. Rationality doesn't have anything to do with this. Irvine is the city where Parental Rationality perished long ago.[3]

Aliso Viejo/Mission Viejo: I have a theory zombies flock to cities not because there's a denser human population there but because the ennui of the suburbs is so pervasive even zombies would become trapped in a mindless cycle of daily tasks and life patterns that would continue unto eternity.

In post-apocalyptic Aliso or Mission Viejo, the zombies wouldn't kill you. The shortage of Crest teeth whitening strips would get you first.

Newport Beach/Laguna Beach: When you think stereotypical Orange County, as in "The Real Housewives of Orange County" or "The OC," you're most likely thinking of Newport or Laguna Beach.

This is where the wealthy cougars reside in their multi-million dollar homes with abounding plastic surgeons and tanning salons. This is where a 16-year-old receives a Maserati after getting his permit — PERMIT, not even a full license! — totals it nine months later, and gets a brand new Maserati to replace the last one. This is where I see women wear heels ... as they grocery shop at Whole Foods.

Every terrible thing you have heard about the white wealth of Orange County festers in Newport or Laguna. Laguna tries to temper this reputation by hosting the Sawdust Art Festival every year. Newport does not try to temper this reputation and hosts the Newport Yacht Club every year.

The majority of Orange County is not like this at all. But people are obsessed with Newport and Laguna because the immensity of the houses and the methamphetamine consumption are equally impressive.

---

[3] If you're looking to break into the after-school education services industry (SAT Prep, Science Camp, Ivy League Cult Rituals, etc.), Irvine is like the Quantico for Entitled Clientele.

Here lie the archways to Pelican Hill, home of the McRichies.[4] The folks on the left are for scale. I took this picture at 10:30 a.m. on a Thursday. The reason I am not at work at 10:30 on a Thursday is because I am an underemployed struggling writer. The reason these beautifully fit, definitely-not-retirement-age denizens are out and about at 10:30 on a Thursday morning must be because they have enough money to be out and about at 10:30 on a Thursday morning.

"I'm not Pelican Hill rich" is a phrase that in Newport means "I may make millions, but I'm *poor* compared to the people around me." As you can see, we deal with very real problems in the OC.

Orange/Tustin/Santa Ana: These cities on the north end of Orange County have historical roots stemming back to the late 19th Century. Generations ago, North County residents rode their horses down Main Street and collected oranges from the grove. Today, North County residents wistfully reminisce about the halcyon days when the living was easy and the world was bright. Conveniently, racial segregation doesn't make the picture.

Brea, Buena Park, Cypress, Dana Point, Fountain Valley, Fullerton, La Habra, La Palma, Lake Forest, Los Alamitos, Placentia, Rancho Santa Margarita, San Clemente,

---

[4] Kobe Bryant is a Pelican Hill resident, to give you an idea of the income bracket you need to live here.

San Juan Capistrano, Seal Beach, Stanton, Villa Park: Cities of Orange County that weren't cool enough to warrant their own paragraph. Sorry guys, I still love you all. Even though I have no idea where the heck La Palma or Stanton are.

Laguna Hills, Laguna Niguel, Laguna Woods: If you're thinking "Whoa, so many Lagunas, are these cool water places?" the answer is NO IT'S JUST MORE SUBURBS.

Yorba Linda: This suburb is truly inconsequential, except Richard Nixon was born here, and I was raised here. One of us ruined lives by unleashing the vagaries of the OC on the general American populace, and the other is Richard Nixon.

Spotted in Newport Beach:
A 10-year-old wearing a tshirt that read:
"Happiness is Expensive."
Yea u rite girl

Chapter One: Jesus Christ

"You know how people say they're Orange County, born and raised?
Well I'm a Christian, loud and proud!"

A convo with a 14-year-old boy:
"God is like Optimus Prime and the Holy Spirit is a ninja."
Soo ... does that mean Shia LaBeouf is Jesus?

Aside from Salt Lake City, Utah or Baptist Country, the South, Orange County, California is your best bet for communing with God.

When I was in elementary school, teachers would ask, "What's everyone doing over break?" From 4th grade onwards, the white kids in my class would consistently say, "We're going to the river." They never specified which river or how they got to said river; it was just a universally acknowledged fact that all the white people in Orange County went to "the river" for vacation.

WHERE WAS THIS RIVER?! It wasn't the Santa Ana, which cuts through Orange County and varies from a trickling stream of sewage water during drought season to a large flow of sewage water during rainy season. No one takes a six-pack of PBR to the Santa Ana River unless they are contemplating misery.

Eventually I took "the river" to mean Jesus. I imagined that every weekend and during holidays, the white kids would go fishing and bathe in the body of Christ. It wasn't until after I had graduated from college that I discovered the river was in fact Lake Havasu in Arizona. *Lake* Havasu. Imagine the countless immigrant children who have had to suffer the stress and confusion of not knowing this bewildering piece of information.

The point of this story is that it is entirely plausible "the river" really was code for Jesus. If you did not practice a religion in Orange County, you were either going through a grunge phase or were part of the speech and debate team and misquoted Nietzsche on a daily basis.

And it wasn't just the white kids.

The two main types of churches in Orange County are mega churches and Asian churches. Mega churches are the famous ones on TV, like Saddleback Church.

Ever heard of Pastor Rick Warren? He's based out of the OC. BFD.[5] Never heard of Pastor Rick Warren? Fie, you heathen!

Mega churches do not hold services. They may call them "services," but they are in fact EVENTS. The band puts on a full performance and the pastor preaches like a rock star. Their budgets run into the millions, with at least four shows a week. Mega churches essentially operate on the scale of a Broadway production. Like *Jesus Christ Superstar*, but furreal tho.

---

[5] BFD may stand for "Big Fucking Deal" or "Bongs For Deities." I'll let you infer which one I'm using here.

On February 13, 2016, I pulled up to the main parking lot of Saddleback Church to see the splendors of Christ in person. Like most Southern Californians, I first judge an establishment by its parking options, and Saddleback excels. I could already sense the presence of the Lord in those neat rows.

The "campus" of the church extends across multiple buildings, resembling a state-of-the-art private university. I crossed a paved walkway lined with palm trees and incandescent string lights. Stars glowed serenely in the night sky. To my right, a couple ardently made out. To my left, flocks of patrons mixed drinks at a coffee and tea bar. Friends gathered on red cushions in loose circles around pit fires. An open-air bookstore, flanked by more pit fires, sold t-shirts and books.

If I were a third-party observer, I would have guessed I was either at a bourgeoisie pizza joint or the OC's rendition of The Matrix. As a first-person observer, I was pretty much convinced I was in The Matrix.

No, we aren't on the set of "Gossip Girl." Yes, we are at a CHURCH.

Asian churches, on the other hand, tend to consist of smaller congregations with mostly Chinese or Korean devotees. They're about 98 percent Asian with two or three white people "trying something new" or married to one of the Asians.

Side note: Koreans LOVE LOVE LOVE Jesus. They love Jesus more than they love vanity, which, considering how much Koreans love designer brands, is quite the feat.

Asian Christian groups excel at eating.[6] The entire OC Korean BBQ economy is predicated on the insatiable appetite of Asian Christian young adult groups. Asian Christians thus worship in the following order:
1. God/Jesus
2. The Holy Spir— Who even understands what the Holy Spirit is? Get this off the list.
2. Food

Now you may be wondering, "Why is she only talking about Jesus? What about Mary, mother of God, or Shiva, destroyer of worlds?"

That's because Orange County is a predominantly Christian pocket filled with fish stickers and "I <3 GSUS" license plates. There are a handful of Catholics, a TON of Mormons, and a splash of Hindus, Jews, and Muslims. I didn't know Judaism was a big thing until I got to college, and the first time someone said "lox and cheese," I thought they were talking about a funky hair treatment. That's how much of a bubble the OC is.[7]

There are some pros to living in such a God-heavy place:

→ People are well-intentioned. I say well-*intentioned* because sometimes those positive feels can be manifested in hateful ways. But on the whole, Christian OCers genuinely want to do right. Clear eyes, full hearts, John 3:16 ink.

→ OC churches do good work for communities. By which I mean they donate a lot of money to organizations that do good work for communities.

→ You get to experience the power of religious corporations firsthand.

There are some cons to living in such a God-heavy place:

→ You get to experience the power of religious corporations firsthand.

→ You are frequently solicited with "Have you been saved? Would you like to be saved?" The answer is "Yes. Lord, save me from this interaction."

---

[6] If you told the Chinese the world would end tomorrow, they would not weep sentimentally or dig bunkers for survival. They would eat until they died.
[7] Here's an even more embarrassing story: the first time I heard the acronym LGBT, I thought someone was talking about a variant of the BLT sandwich.

→ If you are an LGBT youth, Orange County says, "Well, that Macklemore song was pretty cool, but homosexuality is a sin that merits eternal damnation." If you are a queer teen in the OC reading this book, here are a few words for you: You are worthy. You are beautiful. Your sexual orientation is your business and yours alone. Move to West Hollywoo as soon as you can.

And God Forgive the Orange County of America.

A conversation with a high school teen:

Me: "Wow that's a beautiful pool you guys have. Must be nice on days like these."

Teen: "Oh yeah. We've never gone in it before. It's decorative."

Me: "You have an incredible voice."

"Thank you."

"Seriously, you have an amazing voice. Lucky genes."

"It doesn't have anything to do with luck. God blessed me with a gift so I may use it to praise Him."

"Have you ever considered a career in music?"

"No, my voice should only be used to sing the name of the Lord. Not devil songs about sin."

"Devil songs?"

"It's what I call pop music."

From left to right: Gary, Martha, Louise, and Patty. Location: Panera Bread

Gary: "We're here every week."[8]
Martha: "There are supposed to be more members, but someone" -looks pointedly in Gary's direction- "can never do the spreadsheet right."
Gary: "Whoa, what does the spreadsheet have to do with this?"
Louise: "You always mess up the spreadsheet!"
Gary: "I'm an old guy! Technology is not my friend."
Patty: "I don't understand why you have so much trouble with it. Just use Google Docs."
Gary: "I don't have Gmail."
Louise: "You don't need Gmail to use Google Docs."
Gary: "Hey look, this is our time to be focusing on God's word."
Martha: "We could all focus a little better if you didn't mess up the spreadsheet every time!"
-Louise checks her phone-
Louise: "Guys, David just sent out an email. He's leading worship on Sunday."
Patty: "David's the worst! He always does the same Chris Tomlin songs."
Martha: "I agree. He thinks he's good, but he isn't."
Louise: "Do you think David and Hannah are seeing each other?"

---

[8] Walk into a Panera Bread in Orange County and you are bound to stumble on at least one Bible study group. You can tell because everyone is holding a Bible, and no one is talking about the Bible.

Gary: "I heard they went to the movies together last weekend. Just the two of them."

Martha: "Who told you that?"

Gary: "Tony saw them, and he told Carl, and Carl told me."

Patty: "I knew it. I always thought they would be good for each other."

Martha: "It's just a pity because— well, I shouldn't say."

Louise: "What?"

Martha: "No I really shouldn't say."

Louise: "You can't just say that and not tell us!"

Gary: "Yeah, don't leave us hanging."

Patty: "We want to hear what it is!"

Martha: "Okay, this doesn't leave the table."

Louise: "Duh."

Patty: "Of course not."

Martha: "Okay. Well I heard that David ... "

-Martha takes an elongated, faux-concerned pause-

Gary: "Come on, spit it out already!"

Martha: "I think David has a drinking problem."

-A stunned beat, as if Martha has revealed the presence of Satan in the room-

Patty: "WHAT?!"

Martha: "I heard him talking to Pastor James about getting help."

Gary: "Wow. I mean, I guess we saw that coming."

Patty: "Do you think Hannah knows?"

Martha: "No. I only found out because I overheard him and Pastor James talking. Remember. *This does not leave the table.*"

Gary, Patty, Louise: "Definitely not."/"Lips are sealed."/"So quiet. I'm going to be *so* quiet."

-A moment of silence. Louise and Patty surreptitiously reach for their phones-

"I'm setting up the Google Docs now because Gary is incompetent."

"You're missing out on gossip. Did you know David and Hannah were spotted at the movies together?"

"Yeah, that's because I was the one who spotted them!"

"So you must be Tony, who told Carl, who told Gary, who has now shared it with the ladies."

"Yes. When it comes to gossip, *I* provide."

"How come you aren't sitting with the group?"

"I told you. Gary is incompetent."

"That's not very Christian of you."

"Well it's not very Christian of Gary to never complete his church tasks. It's called 'organized religion' for a reason ... because it's supposed to be ORGANIZED. I'll rejoin after I clean up Gary's mess."

"I thought all he did was fail to share the spreadsheet with everyone."

"Exactly. *Disaster.*"

OC NATIVE'S GUIDE TO RAISING YOUR CHILD

But Lynn, you don't know anything about raising a child! True. Every time I'm having a bad day, I tell myself "At least I'm not pregnant with an impending infant."

That is why the person presenting this section will be my suburbanite, debutante, third-generation OC mom alter ego: Linda Lyman (yes, she married a Jewish man, which makes her babies Jasian — half Jewish, half Asian. It's all the rage these days).

Linda, take it away:

Hey folks, come on in. Today, the Parent-Teacher-Student-God-Father-and-Holy Spirit Association is presenting tips and tricks to raising your child in Orange County.

-mild applause-

Life is hard for Millennials. In today's day and age, your child will be presented with many technologies and opportunities to sin. You don't know whom you can trust anymore. I used to think Emma Watson was a great role model for my daughter. Here was a young woman who studied in the library. But then she wore a recycled dress to the Met Gala. What kind of message does that send to our kids? Conservation? We all know that's useless.

From the time your children are infants, you want to teach them how to win a zero-sum game. For example, let me start with my youngest, Matty. Matthias is 9 years old. Let's take a look at his summer schedule. If he stays on this track, we're confident he'll HYPS:

MON	TUES	WED	THURS	FRI	SAT	SUN
7:30 a.m. GOLF	9 a.m. TENNIS	7:30 a.m. GOLF	9 a.m. TENNIS	7 a.m. Fun day! HORSE BACK RIDING	6:30 a.m. Volunteer work at local hospital	8 a.m. AM CHURCH Service
1 p.m. Science BOOT CAMP	1 p.m. MATH BOOT CAMP	1 p.m. SPEECH + DEBATE CAMP	1 p.m. Science + MATH BOOT CAMP	1 p.m. SPEECH + DEBATE CAMP	11 a.m. SAT prep (never too early to start!)	12 p.m. HELP THE OLD
4 p.m. SWIM TEAM	4 p.m. SWIM TEAM (ignore his whining)	4 p.m. SWIM TEAM (ignore his screams)	4 p.m. SWIM TEAM (stifle his screams)	4 p.m. SWIM TEAM (gag him if you need to)	3 p.m. SWIM MEET (1st place or no dessert)	3 p.m. MORE CHURCH (double scoop of Jesus!)
7 p.m. CELLO LESSON	7 p.m. VOCAL LESSON	6 p.m. Music Practice (remind him how much $$ is spent on him)	7 p.m. CELLO + VOCAL LESSON AT THE SAME TIME	8 p.m. Friends Time (to build a political network)	6 p.m. ALONE TIME. Howls of pain are totally normal	8 p.m. TIME TO REPENT

Lynn here, butting in. Matty's schedule is not even close to what you would call "crazy." I've seen 9-year-olds in Orange County do more. And FYI, HYPS stands for getting into Harvard, Yale, Princeton, and Stanford in one admissions cycle. It's a real thing children aspire to achieve by making blood sacrifices to College Board. Carry on, Linda, what else you got?

Excuse me for the very rude interruption. Okay, where was I? On to my daughter, Vanessa. She's 16, a senior in high school, and will be applying to colleges this upcoming fall. This is what her day-to-day will look like this September:

5:45 a.m.: Wake up, run 5 miles, shower
6:55 a.m.: 0 period choir practice — Vanessa leads the alto section
1st period: AP Government
2nd period: AP Physics
Break: Quick staff meeting w/ the school newspaper — Vanessa is editor-in-chief
3rd period: AP Statistics
4th period: AP Literature
Lunch: Red Cross meeting in Ms. Owen's room — Vanessa is club president
5th period: AP Economics
6th period: Varsity Tennis practice — in the winter Vanessa is point guard for the Varsity Basketball team, and in the spring Vanessa is captain of the Varsity Lacrosse team, which she founded
After school activities: Oh, how I LOVE color coding my children's schedules!
3:30 p.m. - 4:30 p.m.: Speech and debate practice — Vanessa is team captain
4:30 p.m. - 4:45 p.m.: Quick dinner
4:45 p.m. - 6 p.m.: Associated Student Body — Vanessa is Senior Class President
6:15 p.m. - 7:30 p.m.: Volunteer at the local library
7:45 p.m. - 8:45 p.m.: Lead youth group Bible study
9 p.m. - 11 p.m.: Homework, self-study for the AP Latin test
11 p.m. - 1 a.m.: Work on her self-composed musical, to premiere in the spring

We are very proud of Vanessa and her hard work ethic. We're praying for the best with the Holy Trinity: Harvard, Yale, and Princeton. But if she ends up at UC Berkeley, we're okay with it. As long as she doesn't come out a liberal, am I right?

-understanding laughter from the audience-

Finally, I want to bring up our oldest, Trevor. He's a cautionary tale that you can't push too hard. We enrolled him in too many things too early, and he burned out by junior year of high school. Now he goes to Cornell and majors in … *Political Science*.

-the audience shakes their heads and "tsks" in sympathy-

As you can see from my kids, Matty at 9, Vanessa at 16, and He-Who-Has-Been-Disowned at Cornell, there are a variety of ways to approach a child's rearing in Orange County. But never forget, the three G's should always reign supreme:

The audience chimes in: **"God, Grades, and Good manners!"**

Amen. As long as you keep that motto in mind, you'll be set. Now I have some time for Q&A from the audience (We might as well color-code this too. I just LUV colors!). Questions?

"HELLO! I am wondering … what score does my child need to get on the SAT to get into Harvard? How many times should he take it? What—"

Okay, hold your horses, mister. First of all, he needs to get a perfect score. Obviously. He should take it up to three times. After that, your child is probably retarded.

"Our daughter turned 8 in April. We have just started her on the gifted kids track at school. Is it too late for her to get into Stanford?"

Yes, unfortunately it's too late for you and your daughter. But if she works hard in middle and high school, she could end up at USC.

"But USC sucks!"

What can I say? Beggars can't be choosers, this just ain't Chipotle.

That's all the time I have, folks! Thank you, thank you very much! Please thank our sponsors, Corporate and America, for making this event possible. God bless! And on your way out, don't forget to make a blood donation to the Ivy League!

"I'm doing the 365-day Godliness Challenge. I celebrate Christmas every day for a year!"

"That just sounds like an excuse to get presents all the time."

"Well you know what all the blogs are saying these days: Women need to love themselves. Because we *deserve* it."

"Has it worked?"

"Yes! I think so. Hey, honey, would you say it's working?"

-He's on the couch playing *Call of Duty* and mid-way through his fourth PBR-

"Huh?"

"My challenge. Is it working?"

"Babe, I'm busy."

"Never mind." -She turns back to me- "*I* can tell it's working because I take less fun medicine these days. But when I feel like being *extra* close to God, I cheat and have two happy pills."

-I'm not sure how to react-

"What? Sometimes a girl's gotta treat herself!"

"I like to do my morning devotionals in the park. It's very relaxing. Sometimes I crack out my yoga mat for—"

-She stops midsentence. At that moment, a dad strolls by, holding his 3-year-old daughter in one arm and walking a puppy with the other. He wears a plain white t-shirt showcasing well-defined biceps. His jaw is chiseled. *Chiseled.* A tattooed cross and "Semper Fi" adorn his left arm. She openly stares at his ass as he walks away-

"Oh. So *that's* why you come here."

-She blushes furiously-

"NO! I come here because the natural beauty of this park is spiritually enhancing."

"Mmhmm. I see how it is. Lots of *natural beauty*. It'd enhance *my* spiri—"

"Get the fuck out of my face now."

-I take the hint and leave her to her "Bible study"-

"I don't think it's relevant anymore to use archaic rhetoric to honor Him. I have a revised version of The Lord's Prayer for the times we live in now. Wanna hear it?"

"Sure."

"Our Father, who are in Heaven, praise, bless up, praise.

Your Kingdom come, your will be done,

In America as it is in Orange County.

Give us today our daily affirmations:

I am the best. I am the best. I am the best.

Forgive our basicness,

As we forgive those who steal our shit.

Don't lead us into temptation, but deliver us from having to mess with bitches who make it hard to function.

For this is your kingdom, in which you are the Khaleesi and I am the dragon breathing fire.

You slay and I slay, forever and ever.

Amen."

Chapter Two: Having a Ball in Orange County

"She likes to shit on poor people's homes."

Overheard at a hairdresser:
"I guess we could go to the mall. There's nothing else we can do."
"Or we could sit in Starbucks and talk for a few hours."

Yes, it's true. The Disney subculture in Orange County is intense, passionate, and frequently terrifying.

Disney has an iron-fisted grip on entertainment in Anaheim. You'll notice no bird poop around the Disneyland area because they've put spikes on the traffic lights, the lamp posts, and other infrastructure to prevent birds from landing and excreting.

In addition to prohibiting avian feces, the skies above Disneyland are a no-fly zone. They're technically classified as "national defense airspace." Disney slipped this provision into a 2003 congressional bill prior to the Iraq War so you, dear tourist, would not have to witness planes with banner tows during your park experience.

During the 2008 Beijing Olympics, Beijing scientists fired 1,110 rockets into the night sky to disperse clouds and prevent rain from falling on the Bird's Nest during the Opening Ceremony. I am convinced Disneyland performs the Voodoo version of this because the weather is perennially tranquil, even when the rest of Southern California suffers downpours.

For those who are wondering, "Well is it really that great? What about Six Flags Magic Mountain or Universal Studios?" Bitch, please. Disneyland is as magical and beautiful as it is hyped to be, and your bank account will hate you for it.

Our proximity to Disneyland has engendered an especially high level of self-absorption in OC youth. We're constantly inundated with messages of "Believe in yourself!", "Be true to who you are!", and "Dream big!" *Believe* may have been the title of a Justin Bieber album, but it's really the tramp stamp that rides across Orange County's lower back. Hence, I fool-heartedly decided to pursue a screenwriting career in Hollywood. My mother blames lunacy. I blame Mickey.

But while the Disney mentality induces hope and ambition, it also breeds entitlement. In college, I noticed the most narcissistic people I met, myself included, were typically from the OC. We all thought we were the shit. We carried an inner security that told us "You are dope and you know it."

Either one of two things happened: One, you continued believing you were the shit and successfully navigated life as a self-assured asshole. Or two, you realized you were not the shit and devolved into existential crisis and functioning alcoholism.

Speaking of which, you too can now acquire alcohol at the Happiest Place on Earth:

→ For $9 you can nab a vodka-lemonade combo at the Cozy Cone Motel in Cars Land. Beats Vegas prices.

→ Wine Country Trattoria in the Pacific Wharf area serves — you guessed it — a respectable selection of wine. Glasses of sangria can be purchased in Paradise Pier. Bomb ass margaritas can be found at Tortilla Jo's in Downtown Disney. The Cove Bar is one of the most popular watering holes in the park, replete with long wait times and a secret drink menu.

→ The best bar in Orange County is Trader Sam's, a tucked-away tropical spot by the Disneyland Resort. One of the signature drinks is the Uh-Oa!, which lights on fire, comes with special effects, and— Wait, what? You wanted something other than alcohol recs? Fine, you charlatan. We'll get around to that later.

Aside from going to Disneyland or having a baby, ways to have a ball in Orange County are limited.[9] They include:

→ Spending an obscene number of hours at a manicured shopping destination, preferably the Irvine Spectrum, South Coast Plaza, or Fashion Island. If you didn't get your ears pierced at Claire's when you were 13, what kind of American are you?

→ Extreme physical activities, such as Zumba and cycling. Yes, I did just call Zumba an "extreme physical activity." You have not seen the dedication of suburban women to their Zumba. It is nothing short of extreme.

→ Downtown Fullerton, colloquially known as DTF, makes for confusing Tinder interactions. If you agree to DTF, it's unclear if you're meeting him at the Spaghetti Factory or his crib.

→ Oh wait, the beach! The beach and samples at Costco are free! #JusticeIn2017

Overall, suburbia is what you make of it. You can choose to view it as Hell, in which stifling boredom and a disinterest in Disney drive you and your buddies to work through a 30-rack of Bud Light every Friday night. Or you can choose to view it as Heaven, in which corporate cleanliness brings you inner peace. Especially compared to communist China, as my parents like to remind me.

Pro tip: Don't become a writer. It sucks to be poor in Orange County.

---

[9] This is why there was an epidemic of middle schoolers who would raid their parents' medicine cabinets for prescription medication and get high in the afternoons. A classic tale of privileged suburban ennui.

From left to right: Katie and Sasha

Me: "On a scale of 1 to 10, how much do you love Disneyland?"

Katie: "15. It's like our favorite place ever."

Sasha: "No, Coachella is!"

Katie: "Oh yeaaah, Chella. They're like tied."

Sasha: "Stop it, Chella is definitely better."

Katie: "Mmm I don't know if I agree. Chella is only once a year. Disneyland is forever."

Sasha: "Yeah, but Chella has Calvin Harris."

Katie: "But Disneyland has our childhood!"

Sasha: "Wait, is this furreal? You *seriously* would pick Disneyland over Coachella?"

Katie: "Yeah!"

Sasha: "I don't think we can be friends anymore."

"Do you think this pirate skull bling makes me look hard?"

"What?"

"I'm trying to get in with one of the Disney gangs."[10]

"How do you plan on doing that?"

"By showing them how hard I am. I can take a 'pirate shot.' That's like four shots."

"A lot of people can do that."

"I'm also gonna swim out to Mark Twain's steamboat and commandeer it. I've been training in the Pacific Ocean."

"I'm pretty sure there's something called security that would stop you."

"Nah, dude. I was born ready. I'm hoping my Mark Twain stunt will let me start my own gang. I'd call it: The Hard Ones."

He tried to commandeer a steamboat. Something called security stopped him. Very not hard.

---

[10] Disney gangs are a real thing. They have names like Main Street Elite and Sons of Anakin, they wear biker-style "cuts," and their initiation ceremonies require new members to break down rides (rumored). If my son ever came home and told me he joined a Disney gang, I would first respond, "Well thank God you have not killed a man" and then pray, "Dear Jesus, please do not let this sweet nerd of mine die in the middle of a turf war over It's A Small World or knock up a girl on a Haunted Mansion carriage. Amen."

OC NATIVE'S GUIDE TO DISNEYLAND

On a Disney fanatic scale of 1 to 10, 1 being "Disney is the Illuminati and they are a corporate empire invested in mind control" and 10 being "Disney is the Illuminati and there is no one else I would rather trust to run the world," I register as a 5 or 6. So if a level 5.5 Disney fanatic can lead you to all the bathrooms in Disneyland blindfolded, then you really don't want to know what you're getting into with obsessive Disney subcultur— AHH SHIT IT'S THE ILLUMINATI FLEE!

Here are some basic tips and tricks to making your Disney visit more enjoyable, from a level 5.5 fanatic to a noob:

If you're here for the weekend, pay the extra money to get a park hopper pass. Unlike Disney World in Florida, which I hear is ~~a giant Illuminati farm used to harvest human organs~~ impossible to get through because it's ginormous, the OG Disneyland and Disney California Adventure (DCA) are totally navigable for a one- or two-day stretch. I've heard of Chinese tour buses that stop at the entrance to take pictures and don't go in because of the cost. YOU'RE ALREADY HERE ~~SOYLENT GREEN~~ JUST DO IT!

Start your morning in Disneyland and then haul ass to DCA by the afternoon. This is because by 4 o'clock, an amalgamation of strollers, tourists, and middle school choir groups make wading through the main park ~~hopeless desolation~~ a Titanic lifeboat experience. Disney has tried to implement population control by driving up ticket prices, but people won't stay away ~~because the call of Cthulhu is irresistible~~.

When you first enter the main park, make a beeline for Fast Passes. These handy dandy slips of paper allow you to skip ahead of all the suckers waiting two hours for a minute-long stint on Space Mountain. However, you're only allowed to hold up to two FPs at a time, so you want to prioritize FPs for the most popular rides, such as Space Mountain, Thunder Mountain, or ~~Voldemort's Snakes~~ Indiana Jones. Then go for other non-FP popular rides before the strollers descend, such as Pirates of the Caribbean, It's A Small World, Matterhorn, or ~~A Graveyard of Cremated Ashes~~ the Haunted Mansion.[11]

When you make it to DCA, pursue the Single Rider track. Single Rider means you don't ride with your friends, and the ride attendants slot you into a car whenever there's an extra space. For the Cars ride, the regular wait is at least two hours, but if you do Single Rider, it's about 15-25 minutes. Same goes for ~~Mickey's Painless Transition into the Afterlife~~ California Screamin'. Some people mind being separated from their friends, but you will see

---

[11] People dump their dead kin's ashes on Haunted Mansion. This is not a drill. Look it up.

them again ~~after you've died and gone to Hell~~ in like two minutes when the ride is over, so calm down ~~sweet child and SUBMIT~~.

The three major night events are World of Color, a giant water/light show ~~that worships Hades~~ (DCA), the electric light parade (main park), and fireworks (can be seen from either park, but show is at the main park). You cannot feasibly attend all three. Ya gotta pick and choose your ~~Kool-Aid~~ battles. My personal favorite is World of Color, due to its fantastic display of ~~TRIANGLES~~ engineering and art.

If you need to rest your legs after ~~walking in a pentagram all day~~ a long day of walking, the Disney Animation Building (DCA) has a gorgeous interior. You can sit for half an hour in the Animation Academy and learn how to ~~summon Jezebel with a Ouija board~~ draw classic Disney characters.

As for food recs, who needs food when you have ~~the power of Satan~~ the adrenaline of fandom to sustain you? Churros and turkey legs, that's it. If you're vegetarian, churros and churros. Keep walking.

Finally, the Disney lobby slipped ~~a potion to Vice President Joe Biden, so he's been under mind control this whole time~~ a provision into a 2003 Iraq bill, making Disneyland "national defense airspace." Oh wait, we already established this. So what I'm saying is they're probably housing Pandora's box inside that castle. ~~All hail our overlords!~~ Sneaky, eh?

A Convo in line at the Yorba Linda Costco:

Man: "Sure is hot today, isn't it?"

Me: "Yeah."

Man: "Global warming."

Me: "Yeeeup."

Man: "Ha, just kidding, that's not a thing."

"Did you get any toppings for your popsicle?"

"No. I *hate* nuts ... if you know what I mean."

"I ... No, I don't know what you mean."

 "I'm allergic to nuts."

"OH! Gotcha."

-She begins to make a low humming noise-

"What's that sound?"

"It's my whale noise. I make it when I'm happy."

"I take it you're happy."

"Very." -She continues to whale hum. Correction: more like whale moan- "It's because I'm about to go on a year-long travel journey to India."

"Cool. For what?"

"I just want to know what it feels like to be alone."

On a Date in Downtown Disney: My Credit Card Has Regrets

My first social media–induced date in Orange County was with a nice Indian boy from CoffeeMeetsBagel. I shall call him Anirudh.

I was a recent UC Berkeley grad feeling lost in life. Anirudh was a recent UC Santa Cruz grad feeling lost in life. I enjoyed hip hop and music festivals. He enjoyed hip hop and music festivals. I was looking to become a writer. In ten years, I would probably end up living under a successful friend's staircase. He was looking to become a doctor. In ten years, he would probably own a home with a staircase.

This meant that if Anirudh and I got married, I would not have to live under anyone's stairs.

Our date was pleasant, but I didn't feel any romantic chemistry with him. He was a cool guy who I would love as a friend, but nothing more. Then Anirudh asked me on a second date via text. I am not one to friendzone a dude over the phone, so I agreed to meet in person.

We met at Jazz Kitchen in Downtown Disney, an overpriced, New Orleans–inspired restaurant. The waitress seated us at a table for two, lit by a single candle. Rain soothingly pattered against the windowpanes. A live jazz musician played the piano. In short, the most romantic setting possible for a friendzone announcement.

I said, "This menu is kinda pricey." Anirudh said, "Don't worry, it's my treat."

He ate and conversed. I ate and conversed and tried to find an opportunity to break my news. Finally, just when I was about to tell him, the live jazz pianist began "It's A Wonderful World."

I thought to myself, "I cannot friendzone a dude while 'It's A Wonderful freakin' World' plays in the background." Well guess what? The live jazz version of that song is NINE MINUTES LONG. After an excruciating eternity of unnecessary riffs, I spewed forth my announcement. Sorry Anirudh, but I just want to be friends.

He looked at me calmly and said, "That's okay." Then: "Let's split the bill tonight."

Guess I'm living under a staircase after all.

"Sprinkles is MY LIFE.[12] I start every morning here with a Sprinkles cupcake and meditation. It gets my karmic energies in sync with the universe."

"How did they get out of sync in the first place?"

"I just sometimes wonder if I'm a bad person, you know. I really hurt someone recently."

"Who?"

"My ex. Kevin. You know that song 'Breakeven' by The Script?"

"Of course. Classic break-up song."

"Okay, you know how that one line in the song is like 'I'm falling to pieces'? Actually you know the whole song in general — okay, actually wait. You know how Sam Smith's ENTIRE album is about how depressed he is because he got his heart broken? That's basically how Kevin feels about me right now."

"Damn, girl."

---

[12] Sprinkles: a v. popular cupcake shop in the OC that charges $3.45 for a single cupcake. In 2017 we are faced with the following outrageous prices:

Cupcakes: $3.45 at Sprinkles

Movie tickets: $18 at the Arclight

Eggs and pancakes: $TooDamnMuch at brunch

Conclusion: God is dead.

"The ocean really speaks to me, you know."

"How so?"

"Ever since my study abroad in Spain, I've just always had this connection with the ocean."

-We stare at the water for a bit-

"Have you ever been to Thailand?"

"Me? No."

"You HAVE to go to Thailand. Promise me the next trip you take, you'll go to Thailand. The water is *so* nice."

She gabs on a little more about Kevin and her travels abroad. We sit in silence and watch the water break. She imagines the waves speaking to her: "Everything is going to be all right. You are a good person."

What the waves are actually saying: "Goddamn motherfucker, we do not get paid enough to crash on these shores."

From left to right: Alex, Eddie, and Jesus, at Angels Stadium

A few rows ahead, a 7-year-old girl dances wildly every time a ratchet walk-on song is blasted through the stadium. She wears a ring of fake daisies in her hair.

Eddie: "OHH there she goes again!"

Jesus: "Get it, girl, GET IT."

Eddie: "Look at her shake that ass."

Jesus: "You can tell she's gonna be hot in ten years."

Alex: "You two are perverts."

Eddie: "Dude, she's wearing a flower crown. Whatchu think? DG, Kappa Kappa Gamma, or Tri Delt?"

Jesus: "DG fersure."

-Future ratchet DG sister whips around and throws them deep shade-

Eddie: "DAMMN! She heard us!"

Jesus: "She mad doggin' you, bro."

-Alex sighs heavily-

Alex: "You guys never fail to meet my low expectations."

"What are you 'Champions' of?"

"It's my hockey team. We won our intramural league last season. And before you say it, I know, I know. I'm like the only black guy who plays hockey."

"Does it ever bother you?"

"Nah, I dig it. I'm the only black guy to play hockey, the only black guy to watch NASCAR … all my OC friends only have one black friend, and that's me."

"You're their justification as to why they're not racist!"

"Haha yeah! Actually, just yesterday my Asian girlfriend tried to convince me it was okay for her to say n*gga cuz she's dating a black man."

"Oof. Dealbreaker."

"Yeaaah, but she's good to me. And let's be real, I got bigger problems to worry about."

"Like what?"

"Like ashiness. Honestly, not having enough lotion is one of the biggest problems facing black youth today."

A Story of Rebellion: No Balls, No Peace

My mom once said to me, "Like Nancy Reagan's daughter, you have a lot of rebellion." I would like to credit this rebellion to a singular event in my youth.

I hail from Yorba Linda, a small city known as "The Land of Gracious Living." It is very gracious living if your skin tone happens to lack melanin.

Yorba Linda, California is the birthplace of President Richard M. Nixon, is the hometown of Cheetah Girl Sabrina Bryan, and was the breeding grounds for Katy Perry's Right Shark. Yorba Linda regrets nothing.

As a peaceful, manicured suburb, Yorba Linda is not subject to much disturbance. The closest this town has ever come to experiencing a riot was in my 6th grade year at Fairmont Elementary School.

During recess, our balls were essential. Soccer balls, basketballs, wall balls, hand balls. Problem: there were not enough balls to go around. When recess or lunch let out, there would be a hectic brawl for the ball cart. Those who grabbed the balls first got to dictate the games. Those left without balls had to make believe Pokémon. Ugh, imagination, what a loser thing to do!

Scramble for Balls was such a frenzy that it inevitably grew a little violent — kids would shove, trip, and skin their knees in the melee for recess superiority.

The administration's brilliant response was not to purchase more balls to offset the supply shortage — this is Yorba Linda; I am absolutely positive we could have afforded more balls for recess — but to shut down the whole operation.

They locked the ball cart and announced we weren't allowed to play with balls until we learned how to behave. No more children would be injured for this foolishness.

We might have been in 6th grade. *But we were not going to have this shit.*

The next break, the entire 6th grade class stomped out onto the blacktop and demanded the lunch ladies unlock the ball cart. They refused. That set us off. We shook the ball cart, trying to break it open. We toppled it over, but to no avail.

We then stormed around, a mob of incensed 11-year-olds, chanting at the top of our lungs: "NO BALLS, NO PEACE! NO BALLS, NO PEACE! NO BALLS, NO PEACE!"

Two of the boys in our class climbed on top of a sea container. We cheered their ascent. From the top, the boys led us in another chorus of "NO BALLS, NO PEACE! NO BALLS, NO PEACE!" Mario Salvo and the Free Speech Movement woulda been proud.

I chickened out when I saw that teachers would get involved. I hid behind a sea container with a few other kids as administration descended on our righteous display of civil disobedience. Others hid in the bathroom. In the end, I'm not sure if anyone got punished for the incident. But we got our balls back.

We became famous on the elementary school circuit. That day would become legendary in YL history.

For it was the one time a group of Orange County residents across ethnic, gender, and cultural lines united to fight for a common cause.

And it is the only protest movement I have participated in that has seen almost instantaneous success. "NO BALLS, NO PEACE," forever!

Overheard at a private equity firm:

"I don't eat shrimp, crawfish, shellfish, or pork."

"Why not?"

"Cuz they're bottom feeders. I don't have time for that."

"I love Orange County. I love the beach. I love the Ducks.[13] I love my family. I could go on and on about them."

"Let's hear it."

"Well there's Akhil and Abhay and Akshay and Akshar and Aniket and Aditya and—"

"Who are these people?"

"My cousins."

"Oh. Carry on."

"Yeah so Aditya and Anamita and Anjali and Anjuli and Amruta and—"

"You have a lot of cousins."

"Hold on. I'm still in the A's. Then there's Aman and Andrew and —"

"Whoa, why did Andrew end up with a white name?"

"My uncle named him after his favorite president: Andrew Jackson."

"Um. Oh."

"Cuz you know, Jackson was a *badass*."

"Have a good day, sir."

---

[13] The Anaheim Ducks, Orange County's professional hockey team, was born out of the 90s film, *The Mighty Ducks*. Yes, Disney owns everything. Quack.

Chapter Three: Lightweight Racism

"I enjoy pho.[14] Lot of ethnics everywhere."

Overheard at the hairdresser:

"Who did you have for your driver's test?"

"I don't know."

"I had a black guy."

---

[14] In this interaction, pho was egregiously pronounced "foe."

Sometimes the hate in Orange County can be terrible and ferocious, as evidenced by the burgeoning tumor of neo-Nazis who brew moonshine in the hills of Yorba Linda.[15]

But for the most part, the racism one experiences in the OC consists of *microaggressions*: small moments of derogatory speech or actions, usually committed due to decades of social programming. Or as I like to call it, "lightweight racism."

Take for example the city of Santa Ana, the county seat of the OC.

Santa Ana is frequently dubbed "ghetto," "sketchy," "shady," and "ghetto."

The only reason OC folk call Santa Ana "ghetto" is because more than 25 Hispanic people and three black people live in the city. If you were to put Santa Ana anywhere else, it would be your average Californian milieu; LA County is chock full of Santa Anas. But put it in Orange County, and all of a sudden it's Mordor.

Q: What's the difference between a black man on a bike and a white man on a bike?
A: The former is considered "ghetto" while the latter is considered "hip." #privilege

People don't like to admit to their lightweight implicit biases. "No, Santa Ana is ghetto because homeless people jaywalk across the street!" Uh huh. Please, name me one major

---

[15] This claim is unsubstantiated but entirely plausible.

American city in which you wouldn't find homeless people jaywalking across the street. Nah bro, Alaska is a state.

Other examples of lightweight racism include, but are not limited to:

→ "Oh you're Asian. What did you study in college? Engineering? Medicine?"

So no, definitely not. [16]

→ "Where are you from? No, where are you *really* from?" My mom's vagina, bitch.

→ "Go back to your country. You people are taking jobs away from my children." Maybe if your children weren't raised by such a shitty person, they would be able to find work.

Now some might be thinking, "Why do you gotta clap back like that, Lynn? I don't understand what the problem is with microaggressions. Okay, so it might be annoying that strangers confront you for employment opportunities at the grocery store, but how is this hurting anyone?"

It wears down on the psyche, son. When someone commits a microaggression, they make an assumption about me, my personality, my background, my sexual preferences, etc., based on the way I look. They take one glance at "small Asian woman" and think "violin math!" and not "football Alexander Hamilton!" Prescribed assumptions and pre-ordained stereotypes do not make for an inclusive experience, and Lord help me if the OC isn't filled with both.

The OC's lightweight racism isn't excusable, but I'm more lenient with these folks because I grew up with them. I know most people are genuinely curious and not ill-intentioned.

---

[16] Picture source: The Internet

They're not looking to cause anyone harm and are simply out of the loop as to why their statements are problematic.

Everyone has their own response. A thorough education campaign is one. Mild confrontation is another.

I have found through hard trial and error that people do not like being checked and told they're wrong. They take it as a personal attack on their worth as a human, when really it's about the way society has preconditioned them to view minorities as a set of stereotypes. People, relax. Your worth as a human can only be determined by God, the prophet Moroni, and the angel Benjamin Franklin. I'm not here to cast judgement. I'm here to gently remind you that telling me "Wow, your English is so good" is very, very rude.

One other thing: people don't change people. People change themselves. Calling someone out in the heat of the moment never ends well. Rinsing them through a progressive education might work, but it is up to the individual to want to participate in that process.

I used to get very heated about lightweight racism in the OC. When someone said "Ching Chong" to me, I would roll my eyes, flip the bird, and imagine their untimely death in my head. But as mentioned above, this gets us nowhere.

I have therefore developed a three-pronged approach to handling OC microaggressions:

1. If the perpetrator is a man or woman over the age of 50, who innocently asks where you're really from after y'all have finished your weekly yoga class, gently pat them on the head and answer their question kindly. Think to yourself: "They're from another generation and don't know any better. One day they will learn. Maybe that day is today. Maybe— Nope." Then get the hell out before they try practicing "I love you" in Mandarin.

2. If the perpetrator is a Millennial under the age of 35, who is hooked into social media and all the glories of the Internet, and they ask, "Can you even see if your eyes are so small?", throw deep shade. They should know better by now. Then manipulate them into buying you drinks because the best revenge is their paper being spent on your liver.

3. Whenever lightweight (or heavyweight) racism gets you feeling down, surround yourself with positive goodness. Find something you enjoy, and engage in it. Find people you love, and play with them. Find a quiet moment to yourself, and take a nice, long shit. Read *Humans of Orange County: THE BOOK* in the process.

Location: Segerstrom Center for the Arts

"We come to every production."
"Which one's your favorite?"
"That's too hard. They're all phenomenal."
"Then what's your least favorite?"
"We saw *The Lion King* recently. I think the cast could use more diversity."
"I thought the cast was almost all-black."
"Right. It's reverse racism! People are clamoring about diversity these days, but how can you leave out white people? What about us?"

Sometimes I think: When Jesus descends from the Heavens during the Rapture, Orange County will not be saved.

"Hey I have a question for you. You seem like a smart girl."

"Sure."

"If we're allowed to call a restaurant 'El Cholo,' why can't we have a fried chicken joint called 'The Thug'?"

"Cuz it's racist, dude."

"I don't get it. Would you be offended if there was a restaurant called 'The Chink'?"

"Yes."

"What if it was referencing a chink in the wall?"

"Except you were very clearly talking about what would be a Chinese restaurant."

"Whatever, PC culture is gay."

1. Excuse me while I go jump headfirst into a river.

2. If a restaurant names itself after "a chink in the wall," it needs to seriously reconsider whether it should be in business at all.

3. The person in the picture did not actually say any of these things. He is a friend who was kind enough to be a stand-in model for regrettable youths from Orange County. Bless you, MakenCheez.

A PITCH FOR AN ORANGE COUNTY-BASED STARTUP

Good morning. My name is Lynn Q. Yu, and I want to pitch an idea for a fusion restaurant.

Investor #1: Perfect. Appropriation is trending these days!

I propose margaritas and chow mein. Think about it. For years, the dish served alongside margaritas is chips and salsa. When you want to order food, you are given an option of burgers, wings, or fries. But what is more comforting than starchy, delicious carbs? Gentlemen, we must change the narrative. Margaritas + chow mein ... MARGAMEIN.

Investor #2: I like this. I like it a lot. And you're Asian, so you obviously know how to make chow mein.

Actually, I won't be doing any cooking. We would hire someone—

Investor #3: Will there be orange chicken?

Absolutely not.

#2: Why? Orange chicken is my go-to order at Panda.
#1: Orange chicken can be the new buffalo wings.
#2: Man, you're a genius.
#3: What about dumplings?

With all due respect, the idea is MARGAMEIN, not MARGACHICKS or MARDUMPS.

#2: MARGACHICKS! Think of all the clientele we could draw with that name.
#1: We get some hot chicks as servers ... Hooter's this shit up ...
#3: Boom, baby, we're in business.
#1: Ms. Yu, you have a dea— where'd she go? Ms. Yu?

"My Zumba class is in ten minutes, the nanny's late, there's no caramel sugar-free syrup left — I've literally lost all faith in humanity."

"Wow. The struggle is real."

"The struggle is *so* real."

-She receives a text on her phone and rolls her eyes-

"Mexicans are always late."

-I grimace-

"What? It's not fair. People make fun of white people all the time, but white people aren't allowed to say anything. Like we literally cannot say *anything*."

-I prepare to engage in my plan of ESCAPE IMMEDIATELY when she calls for me to wait-

"If I gave you money, would you mind watching my kid for an hour?"

"Sorry ma'am, I have to go."

"Gosh dang it. This day is literally going to kill me. *Literally*."

I checked in with her the next day. She did not die. Literally.

OC NATIVE'S GUIDE TO POLITICS

Forget conservative or liberal. This is socio-political. This is OC society. *This is feral.* Read the following scenarios and see how you would navigate the OC political landscape.

Scenario 1: Luke is a passionate singer who loves to lead church worship services. However, he's hopelessly off-key and it pains the congregation to listen to him. The kid's heart is in the right place, but multiple congregation members have come to you, the pastor, and politely suggested that Luke get the fuck off stage.

How do you respond?

Scenario 2: Urvashi is a vegetarian. No, this is not for religious reasons. Yes, this is because she read *Charlotte's Web* once and never ate meat again. As Urvashi's mom, you think this is very white of your daughter, but you respect her dietary choices.

Urvashi's best friend is Jae, the most popular kid in school. Jae always has people over at his house for get-togethers and backyard BBQs. However, Jae's mom, Mrs. Kim, can never remember that Urvashi is on a no-meat-for-life diet. Secretly, Mrs. Kim thinks vegetarianism is hippie liberal bullshit. Mrs. Kim exclusively serves meat-based dishes ~~that little cunt~~, and Urvashi comes home from their parties starving, having snacked only on bean sprouts.

As Urvashi's mother, *what do you do?*

Scenario 3: You are driving a Cadillac Escalade ... or maybe it's a Land Rover Range Rover ... or it might be a Red Rover Red Rover Send a Nondescript, Black, Gasoline-Devouring Machine Right Over.

Regardless, you are driving a military-tank-that-has-been-converted-into-a-vehicle-for-suburban-transport with five children — your twin boys, Mrs. Chen's son, Mrs. Patel's daughter, and Mr. Moretti-Richardson's adolescent, whose last name happens to be Moretti-Richardson-Cox-Anderson. But since the Moretti-Richardson-Cox-Anderson kid's parents are currently undergoing a divorce, he might have his name shortened. Really though, he doesn't mind having four hyphenated names, because the initials come out to MRCA, which he interprets as Mr. California.

It's rumored that dad, Mr. Moretti-Richardson, is in a pretty serious relationship with Ms. Hamilton-Howard, and if they get married, their next kid ... well, God bless.

So you're chaperoning the speech and debate team home after an exhausting tournament, when the Moretti-Richardson-Cox-Anderson kid takes off his shoes in the car.

It stinks. It stinks worse than having to fill out Moretti-Richardson-Cox-Anderson on standardized testing forms. They don't even have enough bubble spaces to fit it.

The other kids are too polite to point out the smell, or the fact that Mr. CA is a stupid nickname because it could just as easily stand for Mr. Canada, and who wants to be that?

As the parent, *how do you politely tell this hyper-hyphenated child that he needs to put his goddamn shoes back on?*

Scenario 4: This last scenario has to do with high school math. When you were in high school, y'all kinda derped around.

But these days, if kids want to HYPS, they need to be in Algebra II in 9th grade so they can do Trig Honors in 10th, allowing them to add a weighted point to their GPA.[17] By junior year, they're in AP Calculus BC, which stands for AP Calculus Before Christ, which would actually be practical in the long run because they'd be learning carpentry. Then they can impressively close out their senior year with AP Statistics and a tattoo of their perfect SAT math scor— what a tattoo no I didn't say anything.

However, Algebra II Honors is no cakewalk, and far too many rabid parents think their children are geniuses and will be the second coming of Ronald Reagan. What the school district has discovered is too many ill-prepared "gifted youth" are floundering in the advanced math track, leading to low grades, low self-esteem, and an overdependence on acai bowls.

To resolve this issue, the school district is administering a placement test at the end of 8th grade — in order to do the advanced math track in high school, you first need to prove you can handle it.

Predictably, the majority of kids fail the placement test. The few kids who do pass are gleefully paraded about by their parents and are that night allowed to attend three innings of a baseball game. But for everyone else there is widespread panic, a panic that trickles

---

[17] A reminder that HYPS = Harvard Yale Princeton and Stanford. Anything less is a disappointment.

down to parents of 7th and 6th graders, whose students will soon be approaching the same test, and 5th and 4th graders, who will soon be approaching the same test, and even 2nd and 1st graders, who will soon be approaching the same test.

This panic is so penetrating and profound, it's unclear whether Orange County has experienced something this earth-shattering since 2008, when a Kenyan Socialist was elected president.

As a parent whose American Dream needs to be validated by Ivy League admission, how can you rectify your child's failure?

ANSWER KEY:

Scenario 1: Prayer Works. When congregation members complain to you about an issue, your response as a pastor should always be "let us pray about it."

In fact, this is a good delaying tactic for almost anything in life:

Can't determine whether the contract in front of you is a fair deal? "I need to pray about it."

The Olive Garden waitress comes to the table and you haven't decided what you're ordering? "Give me a second to pray about it."

This guy you've been casually seeing suddenly pops a knee and proposes after three weeks of dating? "I'm going to need to pray about this. Indefinitely."

As the pastor, draw Luke aside and have him pray with you for guidance from the Lord.
You: "Luke, I've been praying about where your leadership skills can guide this church."
Luke: "In music!"
You: "Yes, I know you're very passionate about music. But think of all the other wonderful gifts the Lord has blessed you with. What else comes naturally to you?"
Luke: "Umm—"
You: "I noticed the other day you were digging a hole to help Samuel plant the church banner out front. You were very good at it. I would even go so far as to say … you were *gifted*."
Luke: "Thank you."
You: "We're thinking of starting a new gardening project for the church, and we need someone to take charge."

Luke: "You want me to ..."

You: "That's right Luke. I think the Lord is calling on you to put your talents to good use."

Luke: -smiling from ear to ear- "Digging holes!"

You: "Elder Mike would still be the main person in charge, but you would be the leader in hole digging."

Luke: "Thank you Pastor -insert your white male name here-, I won't let you down!"

Voila. You have avoided a political meltdown. You have appeased your congregation members by removing Luke from the worship team *and* you have provided Luke with a purpose-driven life.

When in doubt, pray about.

Scenario 2: Blackmail Works. When you hear your daughter has been left to starve at a party, your first instinct is to set Mrs. Kim's house on fire.

But Mrs. Kim, like her son, is immensely popular amongst the moms, and you'll be seeing her for years to come. You know Mrs. Kim is unlikely to listen to your complaints, but she *will* listen to her good-looking, hard-working, possibly Adderall-dealing, eldest son.

The solution is two-fold: You are allowed to gossip about Mrs. Kim with your closest circle of parent friends, which includes two moms and an Adderall-fueled dad. Huh. Wonder where he gets it from.

You tell them Mrs. Kim is an unconscionable bitch for allowing poor Urvashi to chew on bean sprouts all night. They nod in sympathy, promise this does not leave the room, and then immediately leave the room to spread this news to the four corners of the Earth.

Then, you politely tell Jae that Urvashi needs to be given victuals at his parties like any other human being, and would he please let his mom know? Jae's a cool kid, he'll understand. If he doesn't, subtly hint at knowledge of his little drug operation.

Voila. Urvashi will be fed vegetables at the next event *and* Mrs. Kim's reputation will have a nagging blemish on it. Source: unknown.

Scenario 3: You Need Work. You have the option of approaching this situation passive-aggressively, by rolling down all the car windows and allowing the stink to blow away in the breeze. You should probably do this anyway, to blow away the bitterness that comes with knowing you could be the divorce attorney for the Moretti-Richardson-Cox-Anderson case, but Hamilton-Howard is fighting you on it.

What you *should* do is this: at the next stoplight, turn around and ask "How is everyone doing?" Like the adolescent fuckers they are, they'll all reply noncommittally. Casually notice that Mr. Canada has his shoes off and in your most saccharine voice say, "Honey, would you mind putting your shoes back on? It's a rule that we always keep our shoes on in the car." If one of your twins starts to protest "That's not a rule!", cut them a Significant Look. Your Significant Look could take down empires.

As Mr. CA — which you now realize could also stand for Mr. Cauliflower Alfredo — bends over to put his shoes back on, slip your business card into his backpack. Moretti-Richardson better be giving your law offices a call tomorrow morning.

Scenario 4: The Law at Work. This scenario is based on a real life happening in Orange County. The placement test described, along with the subsequent panic, occurred summer 2014.

Since so many kids had failed the test, the district offered a make-up exam in August, right before the start of freshman year.

One response was to send your child to expensive after-school tutoring academies to prep for the August test. The other response was to threaten to sue the school district. Naturally, Orange County went with the latter.

In the end, the school district chose to void all test results rather than deal with a lawsuit.

Ah, the delightful vagaries of the legal profession. Most helpful in aiding O.J. Simpson and hypersensitive parents whose children can't do math.

When in doubt, pray about. Then, in true Orange County fashion, sue the pants off your enemies.

Chapter 4: Asians of Orange County

"I walked into H&M the other day and they didn't have my size. God, I'm being oppressed."

Seen at an Asian supermarket:
A 60+ year old Korean woman wearing a shirt that said "BOSS ASS BITCH."
This is me in 40 years.

Asianz of Orange County. Let's do it:

New money, first-generation Chinese: New money Chinese are *obscenely* wealthy. They collect property in Southern California like I collect ... Never mind. I don't own six of anything.

New *MONEY* Chinese worship the most American of pursuits — the inalienable right to chase Benjamins. I presented a 13-year-old student who came from a new money Chinese family with the prompt "The greatest things in life cannot be held in your hand." He looked at me confused and said "Yes it can. Money." I tried to tell him, "No, the quote is talking about things like family and friendship and love." He adamantly shook his head. "No. The best thing in life is money. Can hold in your hand." Sigh. Capitalism 66,666,666,666; Lynn 0.

Middle class, first-generation Chinese: These hard-working immigrants busted their asses to get to this country and make it to the beautiful, paved lanes of Orange County. They started from the bottom, and now they here, in Irvine, California.

Middle class Chinese are singularly focused on attaining admission to prestigious higher education institutions. All the money that is not going towards the mortgage or the cars is going to the HYPS dream.

One of the most frequently used phrases amongst middle class Chinese is "Harvard," coming in third after "Have you eaten yet?" and "It's cold outside, wear more!" For OC Chinese, Harvard is more than a college, it's an obsession. If you went to Harvard, you will get respect faster than a white man gets paid.

And if you aren't aiming for the Ivies, you should at least be going to the UCs or Cal States. It is a given you will do the bare minimum of earning a college degree and vindicating the parental unit of the American Dream.

I asked my mother what the difference was between new money Chinese and middle class Chinese, besides the money. She responded, "What a foolish question! The difference is they have a lot more money."

Taiwanese: The Taiwanese are credited with pioneering the boba craze. Hillary Clinton famously called boba "chewy tea." People laughed at her, but tbh chewy tea is bae af.[18] Traditional boba involves milk tea and tapioca, but these days, boba comes in the form of green tea, black tea, slushies, smoothies, and syringes. You can get your daily hit at any plaza in Irvine.

---

[18] May this book be unearthed by linguists in 100 years and stand as a testament to Millennial slang.

The Taiwanese are also responsible for spearheading the Asian bakery craze, known for pineapple bread, taro bread, egg tarts, snow, shaved ice, and other delicious desserts that sound vaguely like drugs.

Don't know what any of these things are? You have been leading a meaningless existence until now. Find your nearest boba shop immediately. Even if you live in Nebraska and have to commute two hours for it — it will shift paradigms and possibly drive you to addiction.

ABG: ABG stands for Asian Baby Girl and refers to an extremely basic Asian woman who lathers on layers of makeup, dyes her hair blonde or purple, wears snapbacks, and raves. Any Asian girl can be an ABG, but this phenomenon tends to skew second generation. Do not mess with one. An ABG can ruin your credit score, slash your clothes, and steal your identity, all while being your roommate.

The male counterpart to an ABG is a "fuckboi," an Asian dude who tints his car windows, dances in a hip hop troupe, and wishes he were black. To locate ABGs, visit Boiling Point — a hot pot franchise conducive to Instagramming — or EDC Las Vegas.

Vietnamese: The Vietnamese are characterized by strong family units. If a Vietnamese friend is "too busy" to hang out with you, it's not because they're trying to avoid you. It's because their aunt's husband's best friend's daughter is turning two, and 53 relatives are coming out to celebrate.

Vietnamese families can dress in extremes. Sometimes I will see a Vietnamese family in which mom is reppin' Dolce and Gabbana, grandma is in open-toed sandals and a ratty tee, and son is rocking a BOMPTON hat and Kendrick Lamar gear. It leaves me emotionally confused.

Koreans: Out of all the Asian groups, Koreans have the *most* tight-knit community. Chinese people are cutthroat. They will stab you in the back so their child can get into Stanford and then condescendingly laugh when your child ends up at USC. I know, USC is a great school. But Chinese people will look down on USC because "the neighborhood is ugly."

Koreans are the opposite. They look out for each other. They love Jesus. They love food. They shoot for the Ivies (naturally), but they are more than happy to end up a Trojan.

So what's the catch? Koreans are also the vainest Asians. There are two types of OC Koreans: Koreans who care about how they look and Koreans who *obsess* about how they look.

A Korean man will take longer to gel and comb his hair into place than dinosaurs took to roam the Earth. A 110-lb Korean woman will walk by a 115-lb Korean woman and think to herself, "Damn, that bitch gained weight." The 115-lb Korean woman will think to herself, "Well at least my cheekbones are on point." Then on Sunday both of them will make contributions to church while fiercely gossiping with their friend groups about the other woman's body mass index.

Koreans in Orange County should be trusted as business partners and religious leaders. They should not be trusted to head Vegas trips. You will perennially be waiting for Daniel Park to finish his 50-minute hair parting procedure.

Japanese: The Japanese community in Orange County is relatively small because they were smart enough to camp out in LA. Most Japanese folks are third or even fourth generation, and many have family members who lived through the World War II internment camps.

The Japanese tend to be more politically sensitive, and of the three major East Asian groups (Japanese, Chinese, and Korean), the Japanese are the most outspoken. They have taken up the mantle of making up for the lack of Asian-American civic engagement. Don't get me wrong, there are plenty of Asian-Americans who are politically active in their communities. But for the most part, Asians tend to stay put and let Hispanics do all the work of protesting.

Persians: Chill Persians are down to Earth and hospitable. But if a Persian family is rich, *you will know*. Dad drives a bright orange Jaguar whose reverberations are artificially installed. Daughter rolls around in a Hummer decked out in cheetah-patterned leather seats. Son's facial hair is meticulously faded.

There are two types of OC Persians: Persians who love money and Persians who love money. Really, the same could be said of most communities in the OC.

Wasians: Wasians are the biracial product of families that are half white, half Asian. Wasian kids can turn out looking vaguely Latino and will commonly be mistaken as Mexican.

I have since learned that "Wasian" is considered a politically incorrect term, and NorCal's "Hapa" is preferred. Oops. OC biracial kids have been screaming "Waaasians!" in their selfies for years. If it was offensive, we didn't know or care. That's Orange County for ya.

Growing up Wasian was the shit because 1. You usually turn out extremely attractive and 2. You got to claim two cultures in your background. Because there were so many white and Asian people, it was awesome when a kid got to say "Sucka, I'm from BOTH!"

Wasian kids had it all — biracial swag, good looks, and a lifetime of identity crises.

Indians: Our Desi brothers and sisters might just outspend the Chinese on after-school education programs, which is quite a feat because the Chinese have singlehandedly made test-prep services a million dollar industry. Indians, with similar aspirations of Ivy League vindication, have made it rain billies.

There are two types of OC Indians: Indians who love money and Indians who love to party. Usually, they're both.

The racist stereotype that America has generated for Indians is "nerdy, sexually inexperienced engineer/doctor." Uh, clearly the majority of America has never partied with Indians before. They go hard at the bar. They go hard on the dance floor. Even the 60-year-old Indian dads go hard, much to the chagrin and dismay of the Indian aunties. You think the Jews do it big? Wait till you turn up at an oversized Indian gathering. Chances are, you'll have such a good time, you won't remember it.

Raised in Orange County Indians: A lot of Indian folks in Orange County are, much like the Chinese community, first-generation immigrants. However, there is a firm distinction between first-generation Indians and born-and-raised-in-Orange-County Indians, also known as ABCDs.[19]

ABCDs are the whitest Asian people of all. They are avid hockey fans. They love Chris Evans. They will win the Fantasy Football pool at your office every year.

If you ask a born-and-raised-in-the-OC Indian kid to teach you a word in Hindi, the answer will inevitably be "bhenchod," which translates to "sisterfucker."

In the previous section, I said you needed to party with Indian people. I am more specifically referring to ABCDs, who have embraced frat culture and whiskey and Las Vegas. Especially whiskey. I don't know what it is with Indian men, but that seems to be the drink of the century.

They are the true party heroes of Orange County.

---

[19] ABC = American Born Chinese
ABCD = American Born Confused Desi
ABCDE = Now I'm just doing the alphabet

In sum, "Asian" is a very inadequate term to express the vast diversity of Asians in the OC. Know that when I say Asians, I mean all of the above groups and then some. I haven't even mentioned Pakistanis, Filipinos, and other communities.

"But what about the Hispanic and Latino populations, Lynn?" I know! I wasn't able to fit an extra chapter into this iteration of the book, and I apologize. If you want to write an addendum and point out all the things I missed, please do. Use the hashtags #HumansOfOrangeCounty and #HOOC on social media. Even if all you have to say is poop jokes, this is good for branding. Or so I'm told.

What this book should prove to you is that no one will ever truly know America as a full entity. Orange County alone contains so many subcultures that are each unique and magnanimous in their own ways. That's the wonder of diversity though — you have endless opportunities to learn, grow, and make poor style choices.

So what makes Asians of Orange County special? They tend to be:
More Christian
More conservative
More moneyed
More— The chicken or egg question of the hour: Does Orange County make an Asian more OC, or does Orange County attract a certain type of Asian that is inherently OC?

Maybe both.

Overheard at a test prep academy:
"My mom said if I get a perfect score on the ACT, she'll buy me a house."

From left to right: Vicki and Nikki

Vicki: "This is our *everyday* makeup look."

Me: "Both of you are wearing fake eyelashes though."

Nikki: "Yeah but they're natural."

Me: "Really?"

Nikki: "They came in a box from Target that said 'Natural.'"

Me: "Oh. Do you guys contour?"[20]

Nikki: "I contoured a bit of my nose this morning."

Vicki: "It's not like you would be able to tell."

Me: "What's that supposed to mean?"

-They pointedly look at my clothes. I have a wardrobe of a 2nd grade arithmetic problem. You remember those math problems that said, "Johnny has 5 shirts and 3 jeans. How many combinations can he make?" Yeah, that's me. I'm Johnny-

Vicki: "Nothing! You look cute too."

-I am wearing a tattered Beatles shirt, old jeans, and flip flops. My aesthetic is a mix of California Casual with Unkempt Vagrant-

Me: -in a pitch five octaves higher than normal- "Thank you! It's my natural, everyday look!"

---

[20] Contouring is a make-up technique where your cheekbones can be made to look like Angelina Jolie's via colored dust and blending. I find it existentially concerning. *Is anyone's face even real?*

Vicki: "Omygod let's snap this to Stace, she's gonna be pissed."

Me: "Why will Stace be pissed?"

Vicki: "I'm dating her ex."

Nikki: "We're all in the same sorority."

Me: "Savage."

Vicki: "Who cares? It's not like she and my boyfriend had good sex anyway."

Nikki: "Ooh, what if she tries to steal him back?"

Vicki: "I will cut that bitch."

-I back away. Slowly, cautiously, and then all at once-

"Make sure to get my salad in the picture. In case my mom sees this."

"It's in."

"Put this in the book, so the ladies know: 'Once you go brown, the other colors will let you down.' It's the Indian version of 'Once you go black, there's no going back.'"

"Oh God."

"Once you go brown, your frown will turn upside down."

"That's even worse than the last one."

"Once you go brown, you'll wet my crown."

"Your mother might see this."

"She'll be glad I'm eating salad! Ooh, how bout this? Once you go brown, you'll surrender like the British did at Yorktown."

"You must be a hit with the ladies."

"My bank account is a hit with the ladies."

"Gross."

"That's *not* what she said."

"It was good meeting you, man."

"Okay. Just remember: once you go brown—"

"Nope. I'm turning you down."

SPOTTED:

An Asian tech bro in his natural habitat, reppin' Fireball Whiskey and double-fisting boba.

"Dude. I just wanna make money."

"How would you describe the med school students at UCI?"[21]

"Socially awkward functioning alcoholics."

"Wow."

"Actually, the functioning part isn't true."

-She takes three hungry swallows from her Starbucks. I wonder if it's coffee in there-

"So if you had to give medical advice to Humans of Orange County, what would you tell them?"

"Don't get fat. Diabetes sucks."

From one human of Orange County to another, stay skinny and keep doing cocaine. It's been medically advised.

---

[21] UCI = University of California, Irvine. Alternatively known as University of Chinese Immigrants.

"Gains, yo. All 'bout them gains. I'm not doing it to be healthy, I'm doing it to look pretty."

"Do you mean that ironically?"

"Nah, man. Gains isn't a saying. It's a lifestyle."

-Internal groaning-

"How's it working out for you so far?"

"Good man, getting that beach body ready for EDC."[22]

"Looking to find someone there?"

"Well you never know. Like that song says, 'We found love in a hopeless place.' Thinking about getting that tattooed on my inner thigh."

---

[22] Electric Daisy Carnival, Las Vegas, is the country's biggest rave and a cesspool for Millennial angst.

"This is the happiest day of my life!"
"Awesome! How come?"
"My mommy says I'm getting a tablet for my birthday."
"How old are you?"
"I'm turning seven!"
"A whole tablet to yourself. Wow."
"Mommy says we're going to use the tablet to do learning. Can I tell you a secret?"
"Sure."
-She leans in and whispers to me-
"I'm going to use it to play games."

Smart girl. When life gives you cookies, eat them.

That time with Harry Potter and the Swimming Pool

By and large, Orange County is an undisturbing place. The most traumatic events in an OC child's life rank in the following order:

5. Parental divorce, which isn't even that bad because it results in two sets of birthday parties.
4. Hamster death.
3. Grinding with some 12-year-old sweat ball at a middle school dance and understanding, for the first time in your formative youth, what it feels like to have a boner riding up against your backside.
2. Discovering the true meaning behind "Superman that hoe" ala *Crank That (Soulja Boy)*.
1. Having some hapless idiot ruin the franchise your entire childhood was founded on.

Harry Potter and the Deathly Hallows came out on July 21, 2007, my sophomore year in high school. I was a moderate Disney fan, took little to no interest in Star Wars/Trek, was a bandwagon enthusiast of Lord of the Rings … but Harry Potter had been my everything.

I used to wear Harry Potter robes to school to celebrate different characters' birthdays. I even wore my Gryffindor robes to take the SAT in the hopes it would bring me good luck (it did — I Hermione Grangered the shit out of the SAT). Y'all, I peaked in high school.

The book dropped on a Friday at midnight. I read slowly so I could savor the end of an era. Monday rolled around and I was on the chapter titled "Snape's Sacking." At 3 p.m., my mom reminded me I had swim practice. I refused. Didn't she see I hadn't finished the book? Clearly, someone on the team was going to ruin it. "No one is going to ruin it!" she said. If this were a network television show, that would be a key foreshadowing statement of doom.

The pool was a five-minute walk from my house. I geared up and dutifully made my way over. Typically, practice was filled with kids on the club swim team, but over the summer, community kids would join in to get their fill of exercise.

The warm-up was to do six 50s (50 yards = two laps) on our kickboards. Some summer kid whose name I have since blocked out of my memory turned to me on the second 50 and screamed "Did you know that—

*** SPOILER ALERT SPOILER ALERT SWEET CHILD DO NOT SUFFER MY FATE ***

"Did you know that Harry Potter doesn't die?!" I remember being so stunned that someone could be so cruel that I remained on the wall, bobbing on my kickboard. The next time the Plot-Ruining Muggle came around, I whacked him repeatedly over the head with the kickboard screaming, "HOW DARE YOU! WHY WOULD YOU DO THAT?! WHY WOULD YOU RUIN IT FOR ME?!"

That is to this day the most violence I have inflicted on another human being. I couldn't stop slamming his face with the kickboard and he finally escaped by going into his next 50. I climbed out of the pool and left practice without an explanation to my coach. I ran home sobbing, locked myself in the bathroom, and wailed for 10 minutes straight.

In retrospect, my meltdown was ridiculous and over-the-top. But completely justified.

The next day, I went to practice to confront this piece of fungal scum. He was not there. I waited two weeks. He still didn't come. In fact, after that day, he *never* showed up to the pool again.

Moral of the story: If you fuck with me, you *WILL* disappear.

Overheard at a Christmas party:

"It's a good thing our house burned down because it cleared out all our old stuff."

-Everyone reacts, shocked-

"No it's okay, we had so much junk in that house! The fire cleared it out. It was a blessing in disguise."

Chapter 5: White People of Orange County

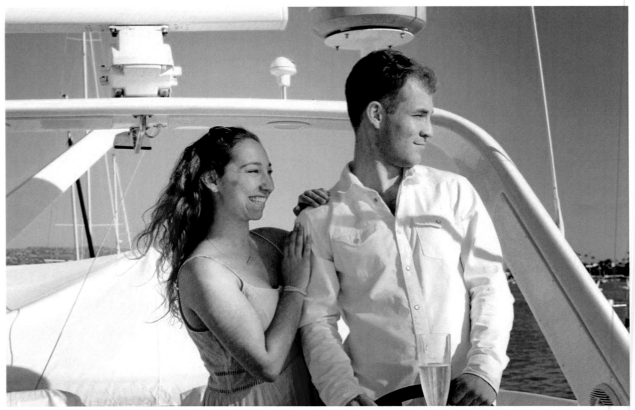

"After I proposed to Kelly, my father got us this boat as an engagement gift."
-I vomit-

A white teen discusses her dinner:

"Sushi is my favorite food. I had so much sushi right before I came here and I almost didn't finish it because it was so much, but I told myself, 'You can do this. You are a *WARRIOR*.'"

I'm going to forego a chapter introduction for this one. The quotes and pictures speak for themselves.

A conversation with a 12-year-old student:

Me: "Why are you late to class?"

Her: -comes in balancing a venti Starbucks and an acai bowl- "I really needed a pick-me-up today."

Seen in The OC Register, a white food columnist ranks the best OC fried chicken by asking:

"Is this better than KFC?"

Overheard at Barnes and Noble, a white teen Christmas shopping for her friend:

"I was going to get you the limited edition but it was $30 and I don't love you that much. I love you like $10 worth."

This is Matt.

"It's annoying how being a straight white man means my problems get dismissed."
"Like what?"
"Like should I keep this boat or sell it?"
"Wow. What a problem."
"Okay, that came out sounding bad. Like I also struggle with being an American man in the twenty-first century."
"Yeah, dude. Should you keep this boat or sell it?"
"See this is what I mean! There are things I struggle with, and people just dismiss me because I was born well-off!"
"Gee, your life must be really hard."
"Shut up. It's not my fault I'm so rich."

This is Kelly, Matt's soon-to-be wealthy af wife.

"I'm so, *so* happy with life right now. I'm marrying the man of my dreams, my sister's having her first baby in a few months, and hmm, what else? Taylor Swift now has a Grammy for Album of the Year!"

"That's pretty incredible."

"I know, right?! What did I do to deserve all this? I'm SO blessed!"

"Not to put a damper on things, but have you talked to Matt about his struggles?"

"He doesn't have any."

"You sure about that?"

"Positive. Why?"

"He seems to be suffering from existential dread."

"I know Matt. He'll get over it with Jack."

"Jack?"

"Daniels."

"Seems a little dismissive."

"Omygod, it's always about him. Lynn, let me ask you something. When you were talking to him, did he mention me even once?"

"Mm ... no."

"Exactly. It's always him first. His problems. His dreams. I know I seem like the dumb blonde who's all over my man, but if we're being real here, *I'm* the one who brings home the bacon. You know what I do for a living?"

"What?"

"I'm a bioengineer, Lynn. I'm a fucking *engineer*."

"Wow, I had no idea."

"Yeah exactly. That's so frustrating he didn't even mention me!"

-I don't say anything. Kelly continues spewing forth-

"But I mean, we're high school sweethearts. We've been together for eight years. He was my first … you know, my first everything. And I really, really do love him."

"Do you guys talk about these things?"

"He's uncomfortable with vulnerability."

"That's a red flag."

"But I'm 23 already, and I can't think of life with another man. I couldn't imagine being single right now. I genuinely love him *so much*."

"Sounds like you're trying to convince yourself into something. I'm just saying Kelly, if you're having problems now, they're not going away. They'll get worse with time."

-A beat as Kelly looks off into the distance, troubled. Then she shrugs-

"Well the wedding's paid for. And I love him. I really, really love him."

-She grabs a handle of scotch-

"Let's do shots."

Overheard at Disneyland, a 16-year-old white girl:

"I need a new beginning."

At a bar in Costa Mesa:

Older white man: "This is my first time out drinking in 19 months."

Me: "Oh shoot, how come you took a break for so long?"

Him: "Ankle bracelet."

His friend: "Embezzlement!"

Me: "Wow."

His friend: "Just kidding. You don't wanna know the real reason."

Two moms discuss their kids. Overheard at Stefano's in Yorba Linda:

"He was mortified."

"Why?"

"His jeans were too big, and Brazilian people are really into style. He came home and spent $2,000 on clothes."

"$2,000?!"

"His jeans were $225."

From left to right: Jake and Annie

Annie: "Take a pic of me taking a pic. It'll be super meta. Like *Inception*."
-I snap a pic of them Snapping a pic-
Annie: "I need to go POTTY, give me a sec."[23]
-Annie goes potty. Jake stares at the wall-
Me: "So ... how's life?"
Jake: "It's coo."
"Anything interesting going on?"
"Nah."
"How long you been in Orange County?"
"A while."
"You like it?"
"It's aight."
"Any Humans of Orange County moments to share?"
"Mm ... nah."
"C'mon. You gotta have *some* Humans of Orange County moments. Nothing?"
"Nada."

---

[23] White people *love* announcing when they go the bathroom. My wish for you is to one day be as confident as a white woman announcing her intention to depart for the toilet.

"Okay. Fersure."

"Well ..."

"Yeah?"

"This one time me and Annie split a doobie on the beach."

"And?"

"We did it in the lifeguard tower."

"Oh cool."

-He grins, clearly pleased with himself- "It was tight."

"Nice. That's a ... that's a good moment."

"Totally."

-Annie suddenly reappears-

Annie: "Guys, you will NOT believe what happened to me in the bathroom!"

Me: "What?"

Annie: "I ran into Leila Pahlavi! Babe, you remember her right? She was on Homecoming *and* Prom Court senior year. I'm pretty sure she got a boob job. Her tits are like quadruple Ds! There's no way those are real. Look, I got a selfie with her. Look at her boobs. Look at them! They're HUGE!"

-Annie shows us Leila's earth-shattering breasts-

Jake: "Tight."

Overheard in Newport Beach:

"I'm giving away my couch. I've had it for two months."

"WAH NOLL."

"Excuse me, ma'am, are you his mother?"

"Yes."

"What's he trying to say?"

"WAHHH NOLLL!"

"Ronald. As in Ronald Reagan. They were his first words."

The following convo took place among 3 girls in about 10 seconds. Overheard at Target:

"Oh my God this fluff. I want it."

"Get over it."

"But I want it!"

"Hey where's your mom?"

"At the front of the store."

"You should call her."

"I want to get my hair cut."

"Ew why?"

"You know microbeads are bad for you."

"I'm going to call my mom."

"Like three milliliters of microbeads are so bad for you."

"Are you calling your mom yet?"

A conversation with a high school junior:

Student: "Yeah this one girl is organizing a group of a hundred of us for Winter Formal."

Me: "Wow, that's a huge group. How are you all getting there?"

Student: "She's going to rent a couple of party buses for us. It's her parent's gift to the senior class."

"Bri and James just got a mountain house in Colorado."

"Who?"

"My parents. Bri's my step-mom. Super chill."

"Cool. Where in Colorado?"

"The mountains."

"Mountain houses are typically in the mountains."

"I don't know where specifically, it's somewhere … mountainous. Yeah."

"Isn't Colorado like a super long drive?"

"Oh James has a plane. We fly."

-His phone pings. He pulls it out of his pocket, checks the screen, and bursts out laughing-

"What is it?"

"Bri just sent me a picture of her and James in the hot springs and the caption is 'Guess who's wet right now? Winky face!' HA! Bri, you naughty girl." -He grins and aggressively types back at her-

I do not understand white people's relationships with "chill" parents. If my mother ever texted me "Guess who's wet right now?" I would reply, "Please never contact me again."

Overheard at Bamboo Bistro in Newport Beach:

Dude 1: "You hear about Jerry?"

Dude 2: "No, what happened?"

Dude 1: "It was his grandma's birthday. He got her a rifle."

Dude 3: "Oh that's sweet."

Dude 2: "Aren't his parents still giving him an allowance?"

Dude 3: "Yeah. Parents won't let him have his own bank account because they'd rather put everything on their card."

Dude 2: "He's got two kids though. How's that work out?"

Dude 1: "I don't know. It's better for their credit score."

-A group of three older white dudes, who looked to be in their early 40's. I hope poor Jerry is their young twenty-something buddy. I hope.

Overheard outside a dance studio, a 9-year-old to her mother:

"I CAN'T BELIEVE YOU FORGOT MY TABLET."

"Nothing beats retirement. Every day I come here and watch the pretty young things walk by ... Drink half a yard of beer, eat a plate of wings, and smoke a cigar. How're you going to beat that?"

"Can't wait."

"So what do you do for a living, young lady?"

"Trying to be a writer."

"Oh boy. Good luck with *that*. At least you don't make enough to pay outrageous taxes."

"Yes, I'm very blessed."

"Boy, there is nothing worse in this country than the federal income tax."

"I can think of a lot of things worse than that."

"Wait till you get to *my* income bracket. You wanna hear my solution?"

"Boy, I'm going to need a yard of beer first."

"Yes of course! Server! Get this nice young lady a glass."

-A few minutes later we're toasting-

"Cheers to being retired in the greatest nation on Earth."

"What about taxes?"

"Fuck taxes!"

-We clink our glasses in salute-

"Fuck taxes."

A conversation with a white friend:

Her: "White people *LOVE* coasters. My parents have like 30 coasters at home. How many coasters do you have?"

Me: "None."

Her: "See exactly! We're very uncreative with gift-giving. I get a coaster every Christmas."

While waiting at the car wash:

A young boy wildly waves around his double edged lightsaber, almost hitting a passing employee. Once the employee has left, his mother looks up from her phone.

"You need to learn how to spear fish."

This is Trent.

"I really hope my ex sees this and knows what he's missing out on — my rock hard body, my 1,776 American flags, my last name. You know, I'm basically Huntington Beach royalty."
"What's that mean?"
"It means we get drunk on boats."

This is Troy. He's Trent's ex.

"Seriously, that bitch wants to flaunt his flags in my face?! Lynn. They were everywhere. You couldn't open the fridge or take a piss without being wacked in the face by flags."
"Apparently there are 1,776 of them."
"Yeah well he can go ahead and shove them up his ass. He thinks *I'm* missing out?! Get a load of this."
"That's a lot of franks on the board."
"Get at me, hoe."

I report back to Trent.
"Troy says to show you his picture."
-Trent takes a look. He's unimpressed-
"I'll do him one better."
-He starts to strip his Speedo-
"Oh, please, you don't have to—"
"This is America, baby. Go big or go home."

Epilogue: A Human of Orange County

I hope you found this experience deeply offensive.

A good portion of today's college graduates have what I term "the post-grad deluge" — we were supposed to be the generation that Innovated with a capital "I", we were supposed to revolutionize the world, but we were met with ... the 9-to-5 workday. An endless stream of meaningless Happy Hour networking events. Discontent with the system, the players, ourselves.

"I watched the best minds of my generation wasting away in line for Brunch." Oof.

I can fall into deep funks. Sometimes these funks will only last an hour or a day. At the worst, it can last a whole month, where all I do is go to work and go to sleep.

This is the story of one of my day funks. On a Tuesday in March 2016, I was having yet another existential crisis. At the same time, I was part of an explosive group chat planning a bachelorette party at Disneyland for one of my closest high school friends.

I coached speech and debate as my day job, which meant I didn't have to show up to work until after school. That morning, I hit up my friend Tammy, who was also a tutor and ran on the same schedule.

I arrived at Tammy's with a mini bottle of pinot grigio, Sour Patch Kids, and Flaming Hot Cheetos. If you ever have a friend consuming these three items before 2 p.m., gently check in and see if they're okay.

Tammy started doing my nails, I started in on my Self-Loathing Snacks, and my phone continued to go off. At one point, my boss called, and I threw my phone down on the table and said, "Ugh, I'm not picking that up. Everything is the worst right now!"

Tammy looked up from my hand and said, "Lynn, look at yourself. Here you are, having wine and snacks on a Tuesday morning, planning a bachelorette party at Disneyland, getting your nails done by your friend, and refusing to speak to your boss. This is the most Orange County thing ever."

I was immediately suffused with an overwhelming mixture of shame, regret, privilege, and guilt. "This is how white men must feel when they're called out on their entitlement," I thought to myself. "Am I secretly a white man?"

Two comments:

First, you are allowed to feel shitty. Even Beyoncé and Jesus Christ have shitty days. Don't let guilt get you down even further.

At the same time, check yourself if you're being a little *too* Orange County. Gratefulness is key:

I am grateful to have amazing friends I can turn to in times of need, who will supply me with free nail salon services.
I am lucky to have a group of close friends who would include me in bachelorette party chatter. (But actually, planning for one is really stressful. Avoid!).
I am lucky enough to be drinking wine. Some people in America, due to religious or medical restrictions, can't have alcohol. You can.

Stop your whining and bless up.

One of my other day jobs in Orange County was teaching SAT bootcamp. I was struck by how singularly focused these kids were on learning to take a test, to the point of pulling all-nighters and popping illegal stimulants. All that mattered to them at that moment in their lives was scoring well so they could get into a good college. The majority of them could not be bothered about current events, human rights issues, or the plethora of problems plaguing the world.

I guess I couldn't blame them. Most OC teens have a hard time breaking out of the Orange Curtain. But sometimes I wanted to scream at them, "NONE OF THIS MATTERS. In the long run, your SAT score *DOESN'T FREAKING MATTER!*"

And then I realized the same could be said of most of the things in my life. Is my career moving along fast enough? Do people like me? Am I getting enough love on the Internet? (Answer: NEVER). Me me me me me.

Moral of the story: We can all be a little (read: VERY) Orange County sometimes. Let it happen. Acknowledge it. And then try your darnedest to be kind and do good to others. Because in the long run, none of it freaking matters.

As an educator, I must present you with a pedagogical assessment of your close reading skills. Let's see how well you get Humans of Orange County.

POP QUIZ ON ORANGE COUNTY, CA:

Name:
Date:

1. Which of the following is an activity an Asian of Orange County would engage in?
   A) Buy a boat
   B) Enroll their children in orchestra, football, and dance programs
   C) Drive to Vegas just to eat at buffets
   D) Visit "the river" for a spring break getaway

2. All of the following are activities White People would do in Orange County EXCEPT:
   A) Buy a boat
   B) Enroll their children in $40K/year private school programs
   C) Fly to Vegas just for Britney Spears
   D) Visit Africa for a spring break getaway

3. In the opinion of Orange County, who is the greatest man who ever lived?

4. True/False: A house valued at $1.1 million is considered expensive.

5. "Sprinkles" is the name of:
   A) A dog
   B) A cupcake shop
   C) Chopped up Vicodin thrown into a Caesar salad
   D) All of the above

6. If you immerse yourself in Disney subculture, you will become:
   A) Soylent Green
   B) A follower, like Vice President Joe Biden
   C) Cthulu's victim
   D) redrum redrum redrum
   E) All of the above

7. The Future Ruins of Orange County will include all of the following EXCEPT:
    A) Disneyland
    B) South Coast Plaza
    C) The Irvine Spectrum
    D) Fashion Island

8. Who are the best party people in Orange County?

9. What is the most important institution in Orange County?

10. Name my favorite thing and my least favorite thing about Orange County.

ANSWERS + EXPLANATIONS:

1. Which of the following is an activity an Asian of Orange County would engage in?

  A) **Buy a boat** — Nah. A convo with a white friend:
  Me: "Boating is such a white activity."
  Her: "Really? Everyone in my family has a boat."
  Me: "Everyone?"
  Her: "Yeah. My dad, my uncle, my cousins ... even if it's just a dinghy, everyone's got a boat." Case in point.

  B) **Enroll their children in orchestra, football, and dance programs** — You might have seen "orchestra," been lightweight racist, and gone for answer B, but you should have seen football and known this was wrong. Contact sports? Please. Asians do "safe sports" such as swimming, tennis, and golf, even though each of these can result in chronic physical pain.

  C) **Drive to Vegas just to eat at buffets** — Ding ding ding! You have not seen someone eat until you have witnessed old Asian grandmas clean up at Vegas buffets. We paid $50/person to be here. We're going to vacuum this place with our mouths.
  Vegas buffet: "There's a three-hour time limit per table."
  Asian family: "Great. We'll be here for three hours."

  D) **Visit "the river" for a spring break getaway** — Asians will not be visiting the river unless it runs through the veins of Jesus.

2. All of the following are activities White People would do in Orange County EXCEPT:

  A) **Buy a boat** — Check. One for each member of the family.

  B) **Enroll their children in $40K/year private school programs** — Check. One summer, at the expensive math and science camp I worked at, a Bentley pulled up to the curb.
  Teacher: "Oh great, I get to meet your dad!"
  Kindergartner: "That's not my dad, that's my driver!"

  C) **Fly to Vegas just for Britney Spears** — Check. "Britney is my spirit animal."

  D) **Visit Africa for a spring break getaway** — The correct answer is D, because "Omygod, I hear that country is sketch af."

3. In the opinion of Orange County, who is the greatest man who ever lived?

Jesus Christ, duh! I'll give you half a point if you guessed Ronald Reagan or Richard Nixon. They come in a close second and third. Zero points if you guessed John Wayne. Orange County's airport may be named after him, but he's no Messiah.

4. True/False: A house valued at $1.1 million is considered expensive.

90

False. Oh so false. A house valued at $1.1 million is basically "the ghetto."

5. "Sprinkles" is the name of:
   A) **A dog** — Definitely
   B) **A cupcake shop** — Definitely
   C) **Chopped up Vicodin thrown into a Caesar salad** — Definitely
   D) **All of the above** — The correct answer is D

6. If you immerse yourself in Disney subculture, you will become:
   A) **Soylent Green** — Possibly
   B) **A follower, like Vice President Joe Biden** — Definitely
   C) **Cthulu's victim** — Probably
   D) **redrum redrum redrum** — Potentially
   E) **All of the above** — The correct answer is B

7. The Future Ruins of Orange County will include all of the following EXCEPT:
   A) **Disneyland** — When Orange County collapses into dissolution in 300 years, Disneyland will remain a center of commerce. The other answer choices are enormous shopping plazas. They will fall.
   B) **South Coast Plaza**
   C) **The Irvine Spectrum**
   D) **Fashion Island**

8. Who are the best party people in Orange County?

Indian people!

To my Indian friends: People are going to read this book and flock to Orange County to experience raging with you bhenchods. Do not fail me.

9. What is the most important institution in Orange County?

Capitalism. The OC may be majority Christian, but if there's one thing *everyone* worships, it's money.

10. Name my favorite thing and my least favorite thing about Orange County.
My favorite thing: That the OC is absurd enough to fill an entire book with everyday quotes such as "The new Teslas are only $40,000. So cheap."
My least favorite thing: That the OC is absurd enough to fill an entire book with everyday quotes such as "The new Teslas are only $40,000. So cheap."

So how'd you do?

0-2 answers correct: Boo, you whore! Start from the beginning and go read the thing!
3-5 answers correct: Close, but no ~~cigar~~ poke for you!
6-8 answers correct: Good job, your knowledge of the OC is complete! Now you're ready to deem Chipotle "the best Mexican food ever" while shopping for a new breed of dog or ferret.
9-10 answers correct: That's creepy. This test was hard. You shouldn't have gotten this many right.

You're probably wondering how much of this book was real and what was made up. Good thing this is the Epilogue, and I've got answers for you.

What was real?

All the chapter introductions and bite-sized anecdotes are true, including making a child disappear after he ruined Harry Potter 7 for me.

Some of the photo dialogue was based on situations I witnessed. For example, in Chapter 1 there's a picture of a church group accusing Gary of failing the spreadsheet. I really did see a Bible Study group at Panera Bread passionately argue over spreadsheet management for 15 minutes. Then they gossiped for the rest of the session before ending in prayer.

All the stand-alone, large-fonted quotes were conversations I overheard, conversations I was a part of, or conversations that were relayed to me secondhand.

Wait, really? People actually said those things?!

When you keep an eye out for the absurd, the absurd happens to you. One of my favorite Humans of Orange County moments was the lady at the car wash (Chapter 5) who told her son he needed to learn how to spear fish after he had almost whacked an employee with his lightsaber.

People say ridiculous shit. All you need to do is listen.

What was satire and fiction?

All the photos were staged. For legal reasons, I was not about to pull strangers off the street. I am extremely blessed to have a group of incredibly supportive friends who were willing to volunteer their time and reputation to this project. This is why the contents of this book represent something closer to Millennials of Orange County rather than a full spectrum of Humans of Orange County.

If one of them ends up running for office, this is the official disclaimer: THEY NEVER ACTUALLY SAID THOSE THINGS, THE DIALOGUE WAS ALL MADE UP BY ME. VOTE FOR THEM unless they turn out like Ted Cruz.[24]

Finally, what was the purpose of this project?

At first I started Humans of Orange County because a quote like "I don't believe poor people should have homes" coming from the mouth of a 9-year-old was too good not to share with the world.

#HOOC has since taken on a greater meaning for me.

The photos, quotes, stories, and guides revolved around a central comedic objective: making fun of self-absorbed and entitled people, who believe the world hinges on their mundanity.

And the thing is, we're all like that.

We all have a little bit of Orange County within us.

In every city, suburb, village, and water park of the world, you'll find versions of Orange County, to a lesser degree. It's just that in Orange County, the levels of self-absorption and entitlement are drawn out to extremes.

Self-absorption is necessary for survival. But when self-absorption reaches Orange County heights, it prevents us from accessing empathy, understanding, and altruism.

Self-absorption in your community and culture, and a refusal to think outside your bubble, is how racism, homophobia, and misogyny develop.
Self-absorption in your earning potential and revenue streams is how labor exploitation occurs.
Self-absorption in your daily trivialities is how it's possible for you to completely check out of an election cycle and before you know it you're staring at the television screen, mouth agape, as a human Cheeto becomes president.

---

[24] If one of you turns out like Ted Cruz the Zodiac Killer, I will personally bring you to justice.

I hope what you saw from this book was that self-absorption and entitlement are not exclusive to any one group or culture.

Yes, I did target Asians and white people and Christians. But self-absorption and entitlement are present in everyone, whether white, Asian, male, female, gay, straight, young, old, or sea anemone.

It's hilarious that we think we are so significant when in the grand arc of the universe, we're just like the tapioca found at the bottom of a boba tea — little blobs of starch that get sucked up through a straw, chewed up by the world, swallowed, and eventually defecated into the afterlife.

The world is going to shit us out one day. But in this life, right here and now,

We have the choice to not be a turd.

We have the choice to be a little less OC.

We have the choice to be an actual *human* ... of Orange County, and the universe.

Stay kind, my friends.

With great laughter, gratitude, and an attempt at humility,

Lynn Q. Yu

THANK YOU

This book would not have been possible without the help of some key contributors. First, thank you to everyone who took the time out of their day to do a Humans of Orange County photoshoot with me. Even if your picture didn't end up in the book, it means so much to me that you would volunteer your visage and reputation for this little work of art.

These generous souls are, in no particular order:

Cory Darling	Tam Meow	Akshar
Bianca Ortega	Priya Patel	Anirudh Garg
Tammy Pizza Do	Katie Malia	Kelly Darling
Sebastien Welch	Teena	Clayton Freeman
Brother Ronald	Larry Singer	Grant Genske
Shannon Villegas	Dana Maier-Zucchino	Yevgeniy Pilipovskiy
Sam Wineman	Oreo	Lakshmi Reddy
Quinn Nagle	Alexandria Oh	Lauren K.
Eric Owusu	Harshita Mehta	Danny Fernandez
Gwendolyn Kress	Rachel Poletick	Kelly Nugent
Susan Trombello	Alisha	Benji Wigley
Amber Morrell	Lydia Fisher	Shane McIlwain
Penelope Gentry	Paul A. Brooks	Glenn Evangelista
Chip M. Clark	Mark Sarchet	Kevin Norris
Eddie Louise	Matt Grifka	Faaria Kalam
Katelyn Kampa	Abhay Mathur	Eduardo Lopez
Griffin Lentsch	Josh Huang	Jessica Clark
John Gaydos	Hooman Hefzi	Josh Fruhlinger

Thank you to my wonderful support group of friends for your steadfast loyalty, your willingness to scaffold my emotional demands, your depthless wells of encouragement, and your forgiveness. You know who you are.

Thank you to Karen Robinson for copy editing, Natasha Azevedo for photo editing, and Ryan Sulak on the book cover and poster design. Thank you to Akshar Mathur and Eric Owusu for the promo help.

An ENORMOUS thank you to Tammy Do for lending me her camera for six months and working around our crazy schedules to make these photoshoots happen. All the images that appear in this book were shot on Tammy's Nikon. She made this project possible and for that she is my favorite pizza slut.

Thank you to my social media family (this is literally the most Millennial thing I could do, besides misusing the word "literally"). Everyone who has ever liked, shared, laughed, or grimaced at one of my posts has encouraged me to keep going with what I'm doing. You were my intended audience for this book, and I hope you enjoyed it. Much love, beautiful crowdsource, much love.

Finally, shout out to Orange County for being the perfect mix of absurdity, tranquility, and suburban psychosis for a debut satire book. I love you and I hate you. Like family, I will always remain loyal to you, but only if I can get in on that Costco membership. 714 out.

ABOUT THE AUTHOR

Lynn Q. Yu is a writer of humor and a lover of beer. She resides in Los Angeles and very dearly misses the free, unfettered parking found at Orange County Trader Joe's. For more, visit www.lynnqyu.com.